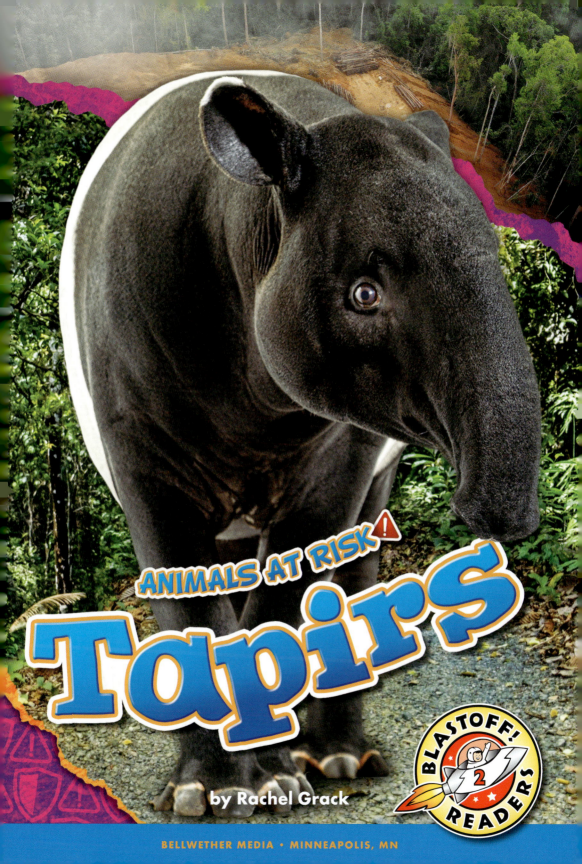

ANIMALS AT RISK!

Tapirs

by Rachel Grack

BELLWETHER MEDIA • MINNEAPOLIS, MN

BLASTOFF! READERS

2

Blastoff! Readers are carefully developed by literacy experts to build reading stamina and move students toward fluency by combining standards-based content with developmentally appropriate text.

Level 1 provides the most support through repetition of high-frequency words, light text, predictable sentence patterns, and strong visual support.

Level 2 offers early readers a bit more challenge through varied sentences, increased text load, and text-supportive special features.

Level 3 advances early-fluent readers toward fluency through increased text load, less reliance on photos, advancing concepts, longer sentences, and more complex special features.

★ **Blastoff! Universe**

Reading Level

Grade
K

Grades
1–3

Grade
4

This edition first published in 2024 by Bellwether Media, Inc.

No part of this publication may be reproduced in whole or in part without written permission of the publisher. For information regarding permission, write to Bellwether Media, Inc., Attention: Permissions Department, 6012 Blue Circle Drive, Minnetonka, MN 55343.

Library of Congress Cataloging-in-Publication Data

Names: Koestler-Grack, Rachel A., 1973- author.
Title: Tapirs / by Rachel Grack.
Description: Minneapolis, MN : Bellwether Media, 2024. | Series: Blastoff! Readers: Animals at Risk | Includes bibliographical references and index. | Audience: Ages 5-8 | Audience: Grades 2-3 | Summary: "Relevant images match informative text in this introduction to tapirs. Intended for students in kindergarten through third grade"-- Provided by publisher.
Identifiers: LCCN 2023036145 (print) | LCCN 2023036146 (ebook) | ISBN 9798886877892 (library binding) | ISBN 9798886878837 (ebook)
Subjects: LCSH: Tapiridae--Juvenile literature. | Rare mammals--Juvenile literature.
Classification: LCC QL737.U64 G73 2024 (print) | LCC QL737.U64 (ebook) | DDC 599.66--dc23/eng/20230818
LC record available at https://lccn.loc.gov/2023036145
LC ebook record available at https://lccn.loc.gov/2023036146

Editor: Kieran Downs   Designer: Brittany McIntosh

Printed in the United States of America, North Mankato, MN.

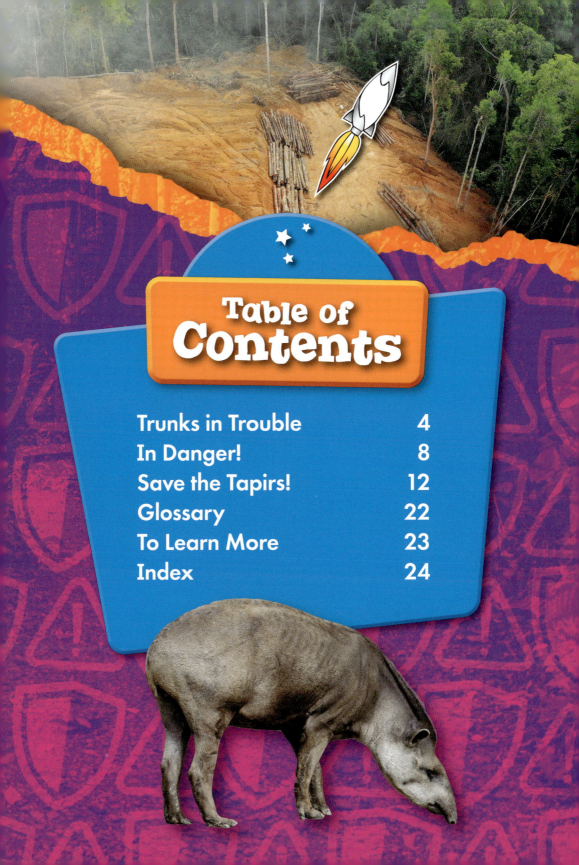

Table of **Contents**

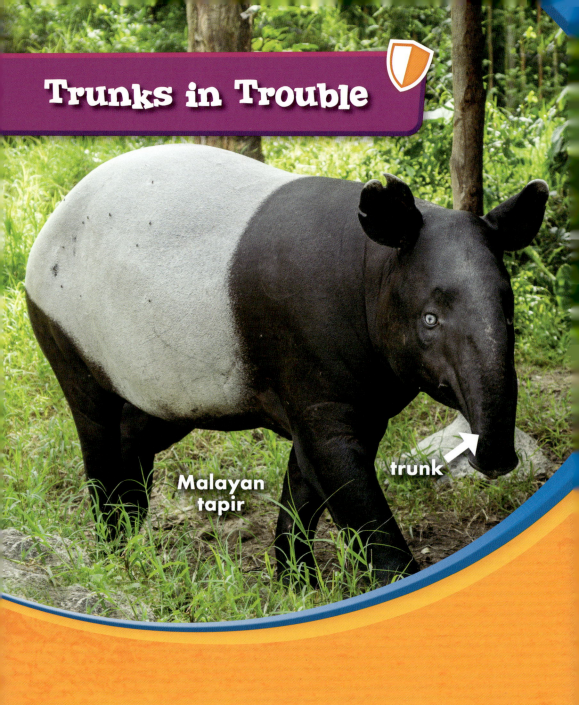

Malayan tapir

trunk

Tapirs are large **mammals**.
They have short, bendable **trunks**.

Many tapirs live in Central and South America. Others live in parts of Southeast Asia.

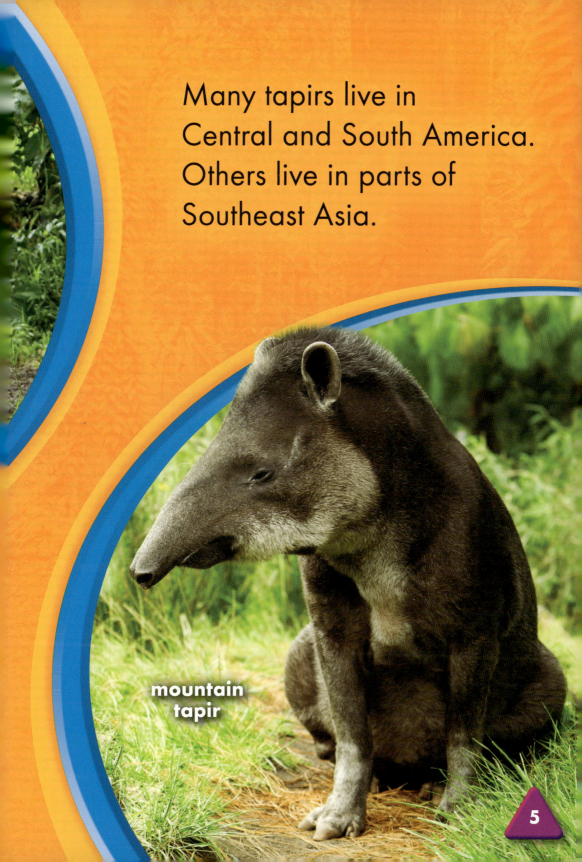

mountain tapir

Baird's tapir

There are four different **species** of tapir. Three species are **endangered**. The other is **vulnerable**.

People cause most
of their troubles.

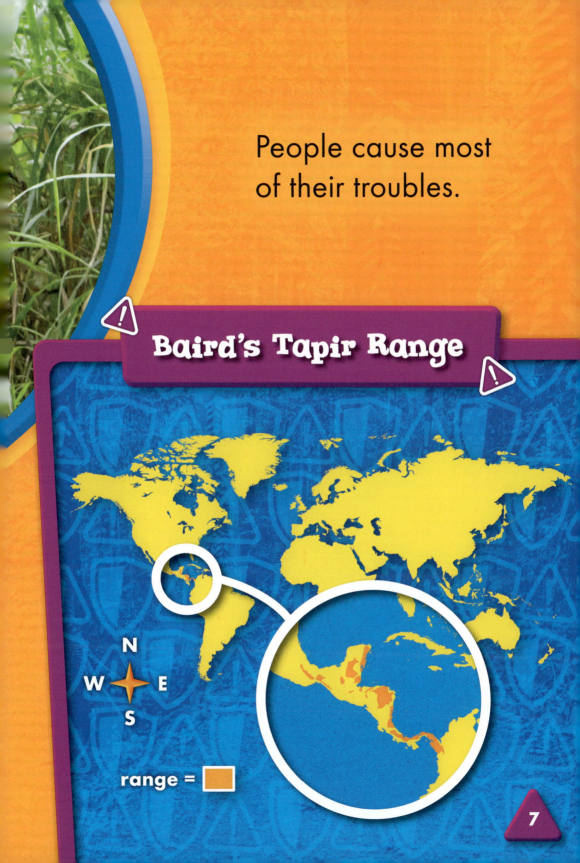

Baird's Tapir Range

N
W ★ E
S

range = ☐

wetlands

Tapirs live in forests, grasslands, and wetlands. But people clear land for farms and roads.

Climate change dries up wetlands. Tapir **habitats** get smaller.

Threats

1 people need farmland

2 forests and grasslands are cleared

3 tapirs lose homes

Tapirs must cross busy roads to find food. They sometimes get hit by cars.

Poachers also hunt tapirs. Many tapirs die in **snares**.

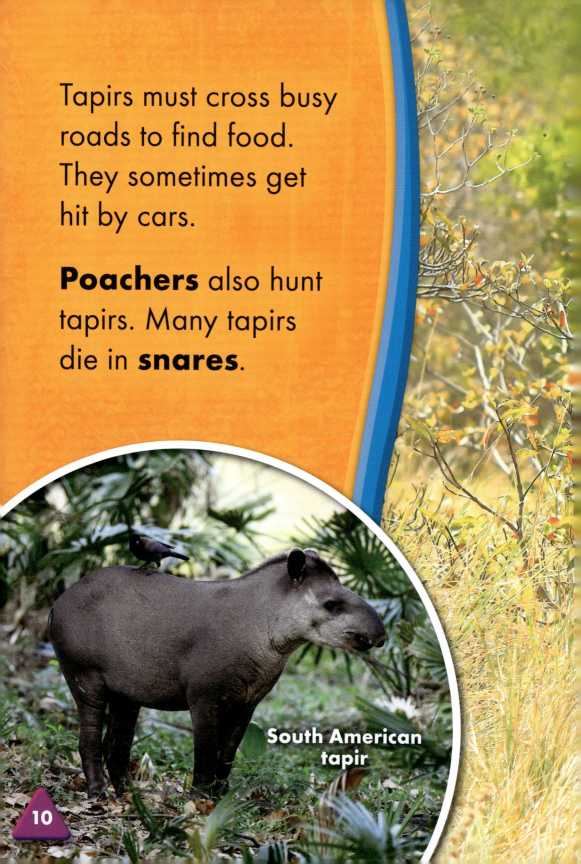

South American tapir

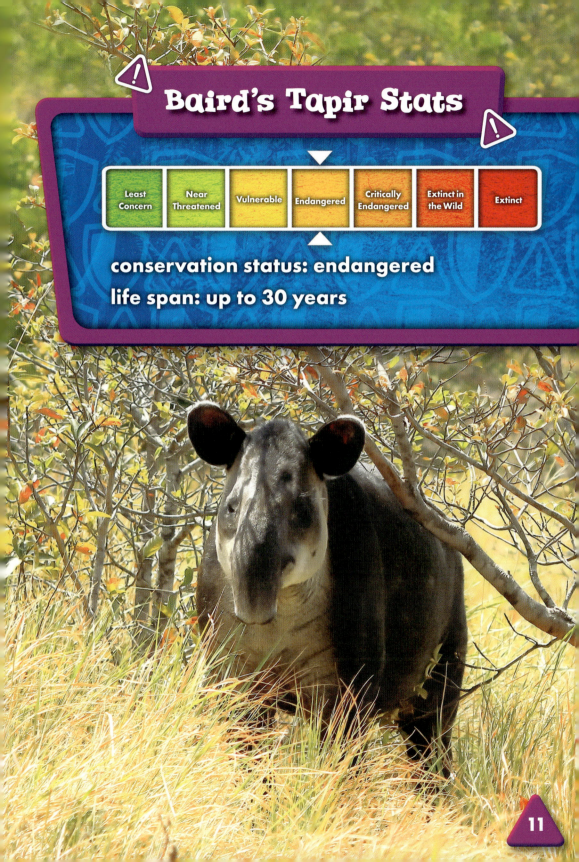

Baird's Tapir Stats

Least Concern	Near Threatened	Vulnerable	Endangered	Critically Endangered	Extinct in the Wild	Extinct

conservation status: endangered

life span: up to 30 years

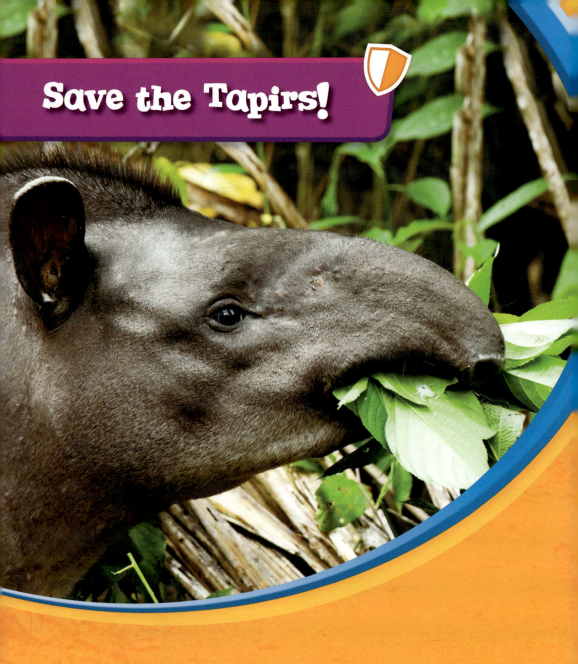

Tapirs are important to their **ecosystems**. They help soil stay healthy. They spread seeds.

More plants grow.
Without tapirs, other animals
would have less food.

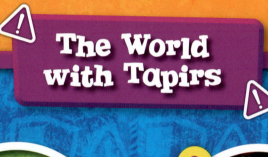

1 more tapirs

2 seeds spread

3 more trees and plants grow

Governments set aside land for tapirs. Pathways between **reserves** bring tapirs together.

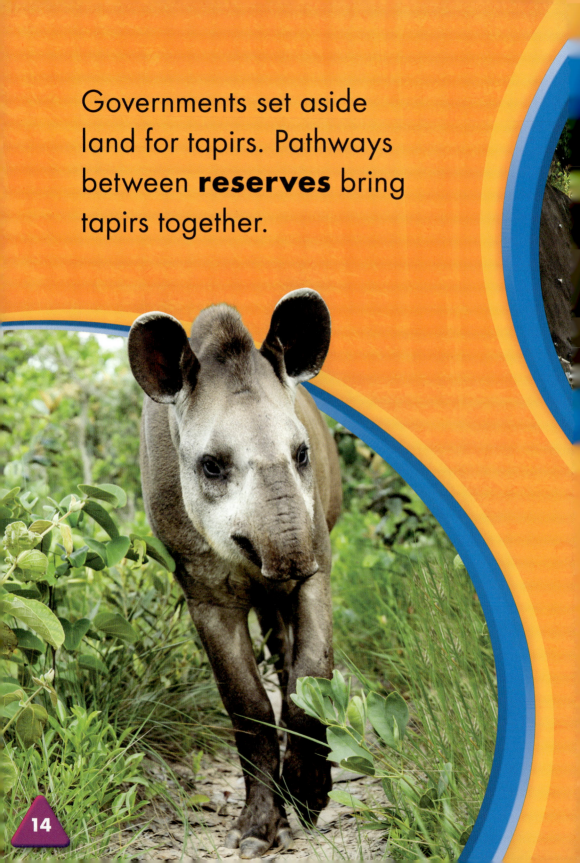

tapir road sign
in Malaysia

AWAS
KAWASAN LINTASAN
HIDUPAN LIAR

Road signs warn drivers to
watch for tapirs.

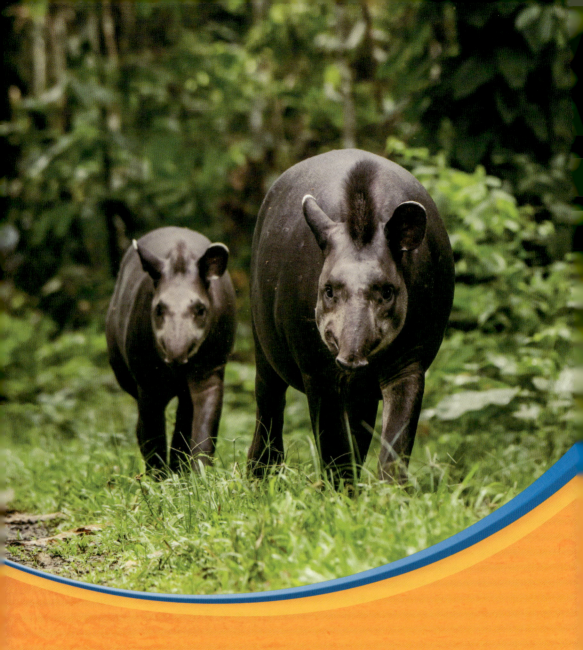

Police stop poachers from hunting on reserves. They also work to stop illegal logging and farming.

Tapirs may one day have larger homes.

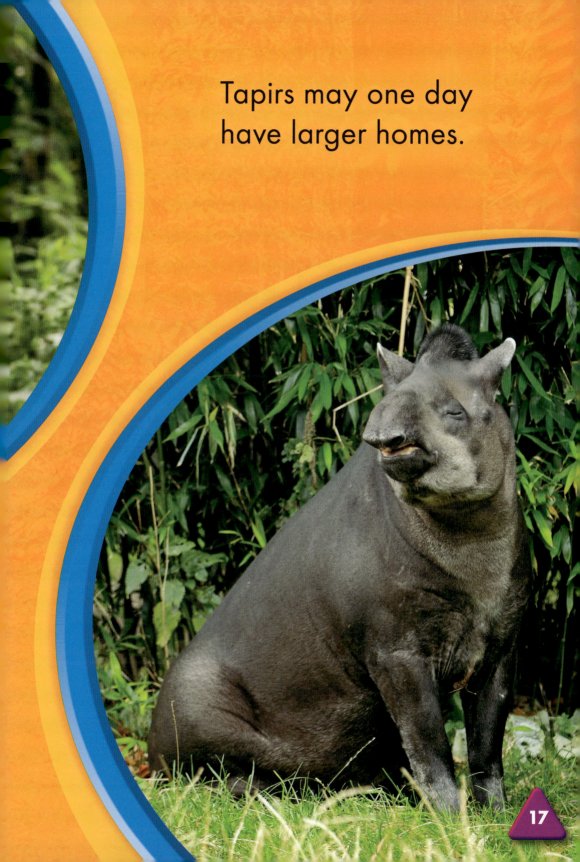

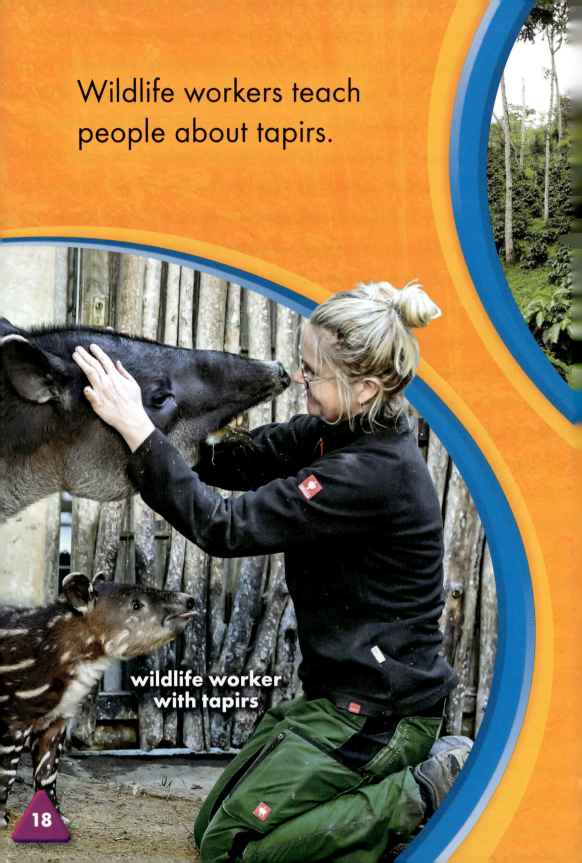

Wildlife workers teach people about tapirs.

wildlife worker
with tapirs

coffee farm

Farmers learn new ways to grow crops. They can keep farming without clearing more land.

Donations help wildlife groups **protect** tapirs.

People can walk or ride bikes to slow climate change. Everyone can work together to save these important animals!

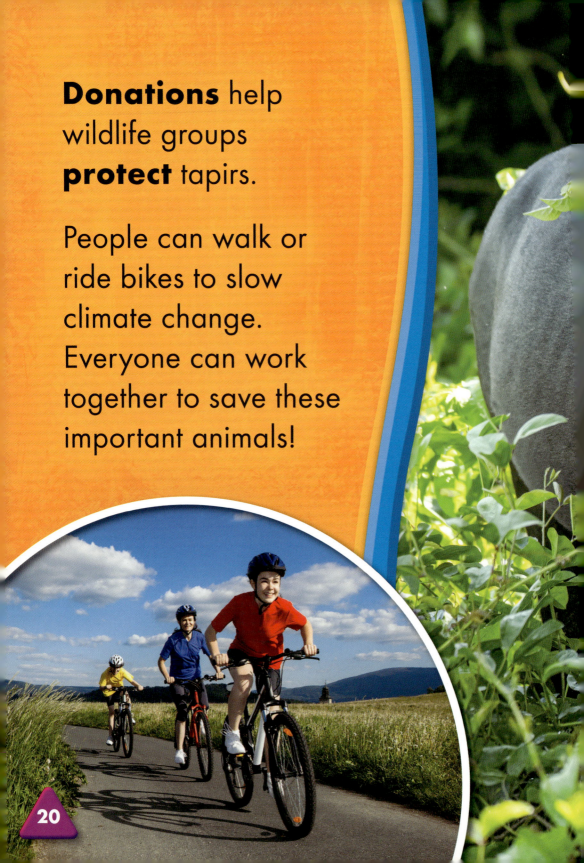

Glossary

climate change—a human-caused change in Earth's weather due to warming temperatures

donations—gifts for a certain cause; most donations are money.

ecosystems—communities of plants and animals living in certain places

endangered—in danger of dying out

habitats—the places where animals live

mammals—warm-blooded animals that have backbones and feed their young milk

poachers—hunters who catch or harm animals illegally

protect—to keep safe

reserves—lands set aside for wild animals

snares—traps for catching animals

species—kinds of animals

trunks—long, bendable noses on tapirs

vulnerable—at risk of becoming endangered

To Learn More

AT THE LIBRARY

Irvine, Georgeanne. *Raising Don: The True Story of a Spunky Baby Tapir*. San Diego, Calif.: San Diego Zoo Wildlife Alliance Press, 2022.

Kenney, Karen Latchana. *Rain Forests*. Minneapolis, Minn.: Bellwether Media, 2022.

Sabelko, Rebecca. *Rain Forest Animals*. Minneapolis, Minn.: Bellwether Media, 2023.

ON THE WEB

FACTSURFER

Factsurfer.com gives you a safe, fun way to find more information.

1. Go to www.factsurfer.com.

2. Enter "tapirs" into the search box and click 🔍.

3. Select your book cover to see a list of related content.

Index

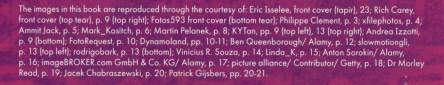

The images in this book are reproduced through the courtesy of: Eric Isselee, front cover (tapir), 23; Rich Carey, front cover (top tear), p. 9 (top right); Fotos593 front cover (bottom tear); Philippe Clement, p. 3; xfilephotos, p. 4; Ammit Jack, p. 5; Mark_Kositch, p. 6; Martin Pelanek, p. 8; KYTan, pp. 9 (top left), 13 (top right); Andrea Izzotti, p. 9 (bottom); FotoRequest, p. 10; Dynamoland, pp. 10-11; Ben Queenborough/ Alamy, p. 12; slowmotiongli, p. 13 (top left); rodrigobark, p. 13 (bottom); Vinicius R. Souza, p. 14; Linda_K, p. 15; Anton Sorokin/ Alamy, p. 16; imageBROKER.com GmbH & Co. KG/ Alamy, p. 17; picture alliance/ Contributor/ Getty, p. 18; Dr Morley Read, p. 19; Jacek Chabraszewski, p. 20; Patrick Gijsbers, pp. 20-21.